SCHOLASTIC

100 Sight Word Mini-Books

Instant Fill-in Books That Teach 100 Essential Sight Words

by Lisa Cestnik and Jay Cestnik

NEW YORK • TORONTO • LONDON • AUCKLAND • SYDNEY
MEXICO CITY • NEW DELHI • HONG KONG • BUENOS AIRES

Teaching
Resources

to Jay's mother, Frances Cestnik,
for her generous spirit

Acknowledgments

Foremost, we thank Professor Dale Willows, who saw the first versions of these
mini-books in 1999 and encouraged us as we developed one hundred.

We thank the students and teachers in Toronto schools who helped to field-test this
resource and the Ontario school boards that adopted early editions.

We thank family and friends for their assistance, particularly our sisters, Mary and Stephanie.

We thank Liza Charlesworth and Scholastic for selecting our manuscript, and
our editor, Kama Einhorn, for her contribution.

Cover and interior design by Holly Grundon
Cover and interior illustration by Jay Vincent Cestnik

ISBN: 0-439-38780-9
Copyright © 2005 by Lisa Cestnik and Jay Cestnik
Published by Scholastic Inc.
All rights reserved.
Printed in the U.S.A.

13   40   14 13

Contents

Welcome to
100 Sight Word Mini-Books!

An experience I had teaching led me to realize the need for a resource that teaches high-frequency words in a visual manner. It happened like this: One day, a first grader asked me to print the word *rain* in his personal dictionary. Just as I was about to write it in, there it was, on the page already! If there had been a picture beside the word, I thought, he would not have asked how to spell *rain* a second time. It made me wonder why children didn't use picture dictionaries more often.

I began studying picture dictionaries, old and new. Most of them were collections of concrete nouns. Some contained a few verbs and adjectives. But rarely did they illustrate challenging words such as *of*, *too*, *why*, *was*, or *who*. Before word walls started to appear, it was a common practice, in classrooms that I visited, for teachers to post lists of words like these.

My research led me to the Dolch list of sight words and several subsequent variations. (There seemed to be more agreement on which words to include on a list than on what to call them: sight words, high-frequency words, primer words, instant words, core words, tricky words, puzzle words.) According to many reading experts, one hundred of these words constitute 50 percent of what children read and write in the early years. Experts also recommend that these abstract words be taught in context. Many have irregular spelling and multiple uses, which make them difficult to learn. They are generally considered "unpicturable." That's why they weren't in the picture dictionaries!

At this point, I enlisted my husband, an illustrator, to help me design a series of worksheets. We started by portraying sight words alphabetically in brief, common phrases and sentences. Then, I thought about composing four-line verses so that children could recite the sight words in a chant, for example, "See that hamster? See that dog? See that fish? See that frog?" The repetition, rhythm, and rhyme, together with the pictures, would make the lessons fun and more memorable.

In 1998, I noticed teachers adding word walls to their classrooms. Word walls are valuable tools because they give children exposure to sight words. But some children require more support than letters alone can provide. Like training wheels on a bike or water wings in a pool, picture cues can help children until they are ready to ride off to, or dive into, literacy. We decided to format the illustrated verses as reproducible booklets. Our goal was to produce a series of one hundred lessons. I took these mini-books into several primary classrooms and got an enthusiastic response. Even children with reading difficulties felt successful because the booklets were only four lines long, highly repetitive, and had close picture-text match.

So, here are our 100 mini-books! You will find instructions for assembling the books below, and on pages 6–11, teaching tips for introducing them to children, as well as activities and ideas to extend learning. May these lessons be the keys your children use to unlock the English language and a lifetime of learning!

Using This Book

Making the Mini-Books:

1. Make a single-sided photocopy of the four-panel mini-book page for each child. (Enlarge the pages, if desired.)

2. Fold each photocopy into a four-page book so that the large focus sight word and write-on lines are on the front cover and the word search is on the back.

3. Also prepare an enlarged version of one of the books to use as a teaching aid when introducing the mini-books to your class. Enlarge each of the mini-book pages by 200%. Use a glue stick to affix the cover and the first page back to back. Repeat with the second page and the back cover. Place the pages together and glue or staple along the left-hand side. Trace or print the focus sight word on the second, third, and fourth lines of the verse.

Mini-Book Tips

- When you introduce the mini-books to your class the first few times, distribute them already folded. At the next stage, try pre-creasing the pages, and then distribute them flat. This will give children a model until they are able to fold the books on their own.

- Let each child make two copies of each book—one for school and the other for home! Give each child a resealable plastic bag or square tissue box for storing their books.

Introducing the Mini-Books:

1. Display the cover of the enlarged book (see Making the Mini-Books page 5), for example, the "are" book on page 38. Say, *Today we are going to talk about the word "are." What letters are in this word? Let's think of some ways we can use this word. How might you use it in a sentence?*

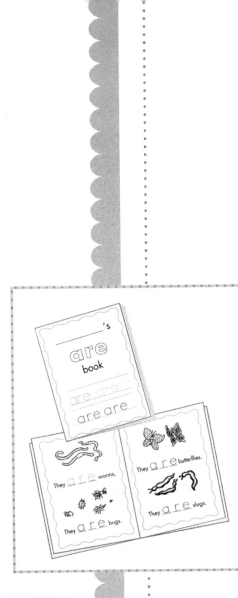

2. Look at and discuss the pictures. Point out how one letter is printed on each dash (*a r e*). Talk about the directionality of the text (left side, top to bottom, right side, top to bottom). Read the phrases or sentences aloud as children follow along. Then invite a pair of children to read the four lines of the verse aloud.

3. Lead the class in a chant:

> Read the word.
> (*are*)
>
> Spell the word.
> (*a-r-e*)
>
> Point to and read the
> word in each line.
> (*are . . . are . . . are . . . are*)
>
> Read the verse.
> (*They are worms. They are bugs.*
> *They are butterflies. They are slugs.*)
>
> Read the word again.
> (*ARE!*)

4. Invite children to use their finger to "write" the sight word in the air.

5. Tell children to write their name on the cover of their book.

6. Ask them to read aloud with you the large sight word on the cover. Then invite children to color the word creatively or according to a pattern. For example, they might color vowels red and consonants blue, or long vowels red and short vowels yellow. Silent letters might remain uncolored.

7. Direct children to use a pencil to trace the sight word printed near the bottom of the cover. (For extra practice, children might write the word a few times using different-colored pencils, crayons, or thin markers.)

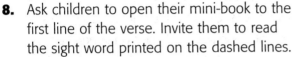

8. Ask children to open their mini-book to the first line of the verse. Invite them to read the sight word printed on the dashed lines. Then direct them to use a pencil to trace the sight word printed on the dashed lines in the second line. Finally, have them print the letters of the sight word on each of the dashed lines in the third and fourth lines of the verse.

9. Read aloud the verse, then invite children to join in as you read it again. Encourage children to use the pictures to help them read the words.

10. Have children turn to the word search on the back cover. Ask them to study the letters carefully. Then say, *How many times can you find the sight word are?* Challenge children to circle the word each time they find it. For Level One and Two words, tell them that they should circle the word only if it is printed left to right and top to bottom. This reinforces directionality of text. Levels Three and Four include words printed on the diagonal, beginning with the word search for "found" on page 67, to give students who are ready an extra challenge.

11. Invite children to use colored pencils or thin markers to color the pictures in their mini-book, if they like. Encourage them to reread their mini-books often, at school and at home, to family members and friends.

beginning with the word search for "found" on page 67

Teaching Tip

As an extra challenge, tell children to unfold their mini-book to the blank side. Invite them to think of a picture to draw that they can describe using the sight word. Help them write a new phrase or sentence using the word.

About the Word Searches

In each Level One word search, the sight word is hidden four times. It is hidden six times in Level Two, eight times in Level Three, and ten times in Level Four books.

7

The Sight Words

We compared several lists of high-frequency and sight words (Dolch; Edward Fry; Otto & Stallard; Ves Thomas; Clay & Watson; Bodrova, Leong & Semenov; and others). Some of these lists are based on general usage. Some focus on usage by children or by authors of children's reading material. Others are organized for instruction according to reading ability.

The most important words appear prominently on all lists, though the ranking varies. We selected and sorted one hundred of these words into four levels depending upon difficulty of spelling or usage. Except for *one* and *two*, we did not choose nouns, colors, or numbers for our list. Most of those words are easy to represent. Many appear in our verses as content words. To compose verses, we matched the sight words with common word families that were ranked according to complexity (short vowels, long vowels, blends, irregulars).

The first level, for early emergent readers, features lessons in a specific order for 25 of the most useful high-frequency words. Most of these are used in phrases or sentences of just two or three words. The remaining 75 mini-books are divided into three progressive sections. The books in these three levels are organized alphabetically.

Lessons are intended to be taught one level at a time because they incorporate vocabulary and word families previously learned. Nonetheless, you can introduce words in an order that supplements your reading program.

Level 1

a	my	see	is	of
the	me	we	to	her
I	how	he	in	his
am	can	she	this	they
and	you	it	that	all

Level 2

are	eat	keep	or	take
at	for	like	put	us
be	get	make	read	very
by	go	no	saw	was
do	it's	off	so	your

Level 3

an	from	look	our	want
as	had	made	said	went
come	has	not	some	what
did	into	now	two	will
found	know	one	use	with

Level 4

about	don't	if	them	when
after	give	its	then	where
because	goes	just	there	who
before	have	than	too	why
does	here	their	were	would

Activities & Extensions

Alphabet Sort

Have children select four or more mini-books randomly and sort the sight words into alphabetical order. This promotes skills for early dictionary use. Children can also take words from a single verse and sort them alphabetically on paper.

Show Me the Vowels

Print a sight word verse on the blackboard or chart paper with all the vowels missing. Invite children to print one or more vowels until the phrases or sentences are completed.

Sight Word Rhyming Time

Make a list of words that rhyme with the sight word and are spelled in a similar manner. (For instance, *get* rhymes with *pet, vet, wet, net, set, let, met.*) Point out rhyming words that are spelled differently than the sight word (for instance, *of* rhymes with *love, glove, above, shove; said* rhymes with *bed, red, fed, bread, head*). Use the rhyming words in the verse to start a list of simple sentences (for instance, *Dad is not mad. Dad is glad*).

Flashcard Mini-Books

The sight word mini-books can be helpful as assessment tools. Use the covers as flashcards. If a child cannot read the large sight word, open the mini-book to provide a picture clue.

Pattern Writing

Unfold a mini-book and turn to the blank side. Use the sight word and the pattern of the verse to create new phrases and sentences. For instance, *make: He can make a mask. She can make a sandwich. He can make a snowman. She can make a speech. He can make a nest. She can make a vest.* This is an excellent way to reinforce a sight word and give strong writing support. It also helps children to reread what they have written. In addition, pattern writing may provide opportunities to discuss colloquial phrases that use the sight words.

Sight Word Shapes

This art activity helps a child recognize and recall the shape and features of a word. Enlarge and photocopy the large sight word on the cover. Cut it out and glue it in the middle of a horizontal sheet of paper. Make a copy for each child. Then invite children to use different colors of crayon, colored pencil, or marker to trace around the outline of the sight word again and again until they reach the edge of the paper. They can also make patterns in the space between the lines.

Visual Literacy

Teach both sides of the brain! Discussing the illustrations can be a part of any lesson. Ask questions like these:

- *How are the four pictures in the verse similar to another? How are they different?*
- *Are some things in the drawings farther away than others?*
- *What shapes do you see in the pictures?*

Connect the Sight Words

After covering most of the lessons, use the mini-books to make pocket chart sentences composed of as many sight words as possible. On index cards, print any extra words that children request. Score each sentence by giving a point for each different sight word used. Do examples as a class, then divide into teams. Determine a time limit for teams to compose their entries.

Scoring examples:

She can do it. (4 points)

Look at that dog *in the* window. (5 points)

What do they do with all the bottles? (6 points)

My two friends *are* going *to the* zoo *and I want to go* too. (11 points)

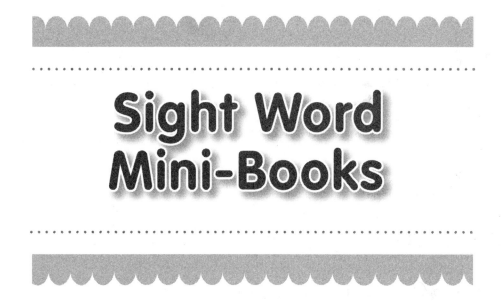

Sight Word Mini-Books

I _ _ _ _ stop.

I _ _ _ _ ride.

I ⌐⌐⌐ hop.

I can run.

Word Search

can

c	a	n	f	a
a	h	e	c	o
n	g	c	a	u
c	v	q	n	d
t	u	c	a	n

I found **can** __4__ times.

(number)

100 Sight Word Mini-Books   Scholastic Teaching Resources

_____'s

can
book

can can

I say, _____ _____ _____ stay!

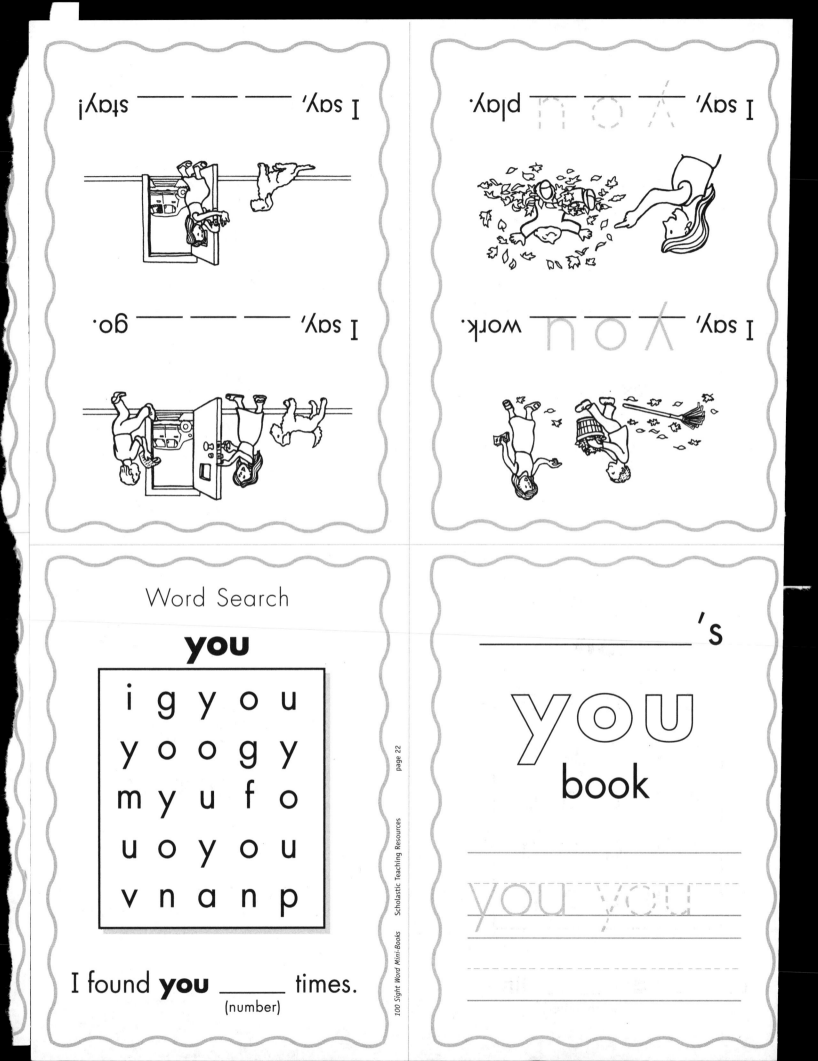

I say, _____ _____ _____ go.

I say, Y O U play.

I say, Y O U work.

Word Search

you

i	g	y	o	u
y	o	o	g	y
m	y	u	f	o
u	o	y	o	u
v	n	a	n	p

I found **you** _____ times.
(number)

_____'s

you
book

_____

you you

_____

Can you ___ ___ ___ me?

Can you ___ ___ ___ the beach?

Can you s e e the sea?

Can you s e e the ship?

Word Search

see

s	e	e	v	s
d	a	p	m	e
s	n	c	e	e
e	e	s	k	o
e	h	s	e	e

I found **see** _____ times.
(number)

_____'s

see

book

see see

100 Sight Word Mini-Books   Scholastic Teaching Resources

Oh, how —— —— clap!

Oh, how —— —— laugh!

Oh, how we —— sing!

Oh, how we —— snap!

Word Search

we

a	v	s	b	w
w	s	y	a	e
e	x	m	w	e
r	j	v	i	f
u	w	e	z	s

I found **we** _____ times.
(number)

_____'s

we
book

we   we

100 Sight Word Mini-Books   Scholastic Teaching Resources

See how ___ ___ hits.

See how ___ swings.

See how he sits.

See how he stands.

Word Search

he

o	h	e	s	m
k	u	h	e	o
e	h	o	n	s
p	e	d	h	i
m	s	n	e	l

I found **he** _____ times.
(number)

_____'s

he

book

he he

See how ___ ___ bikes.

See how ___ kicks.

See how she hikes.

See how she skates.

Word Search

she

s	n	c	s	q
h	o	s	h	e
e	h	i	e	s
f	e	s	h	l
c	s	h	e	w

I found **she** _____ times.
(number)

_____'s

she
book

she she

How well _____ talks!

Hello!

How well _____ rocks!

How well __i__t__ walks!

How well __i__t__ rolls!

Word Search

it

e	t	p	f	y
l	a	i	t	z
b	k	i	x	r
f	u	t	g	i
i	t	l	m	t

I found **it** _____ times.
(number)

_____'s

i t

book

i t   i t

It ___ a lot!

It ___ good.

It is hot.

It is sunny.

Word Search

is

d	i	u	e	l
r	s	n	b	i
i	z	j	m	s
a	i	s	w	o
f	e	i	s	h

I found **is** _____ times.
(number)

_____'s

is

book

is   is

_____ the store

_____ the mall

to _____ the shore

to _____ the mountain

Word Search

to

s	d	a	c	f
o	y	t	t	o
e	q	o	s	t
t	o	a	p	o
h	x	c	k	v

I found **to** _____ times.
(number)

_____'s

to book

to to

___ the car

___ the cup

in the jar

in the box

Word Search

in

i	n	f	j	n
h	i	r	i	m
f	u	z	n	y
o	i	u	m	c
i	n	e	i	h

I found **in** _____ times.
(number)

_____'s

in
book

in in

And —————
is my brother.

And —————
is my sister.

And t h i s
is my mother.

See, this
is my father.

Word Search

this

p	t	h	i	t
n	f	i	t	h
i	h	w	h	i
s	t	h	i	s
t	h	i	s	t

I found **this** _____ times.
(number)

_____'s

t h i s

book

this this

See ___ dog?

See ___ snake?

See that frog?

See that hamster?

Word Search

that

e	t	b	w	t
t	h	a	t	h
l	a	q	f	a
s	t	h	a	t
h	a	u	m	e

I found **that** _____ times.
(number)

_____'s

that

book

that that

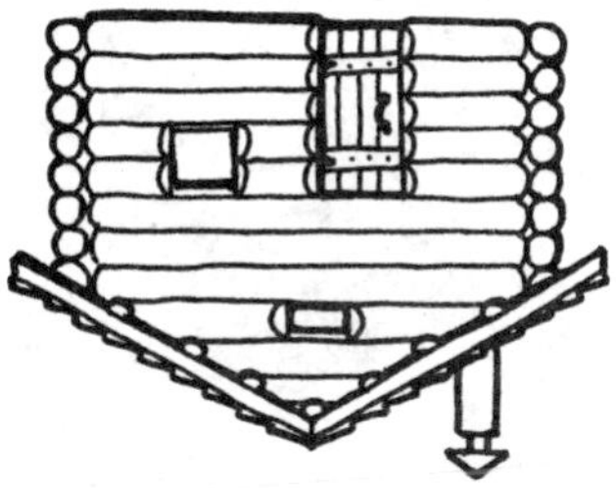

a house ___ ___ logs

a house ___ ___ bricks

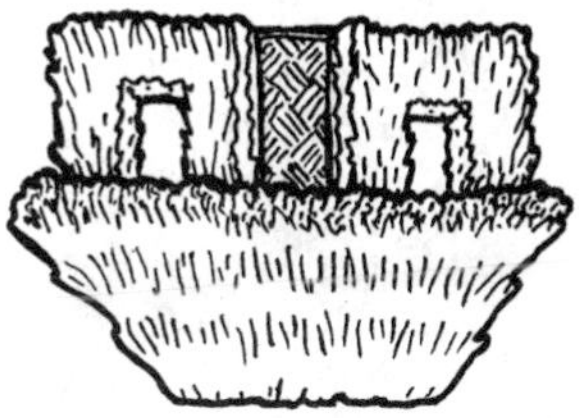

a house of straw

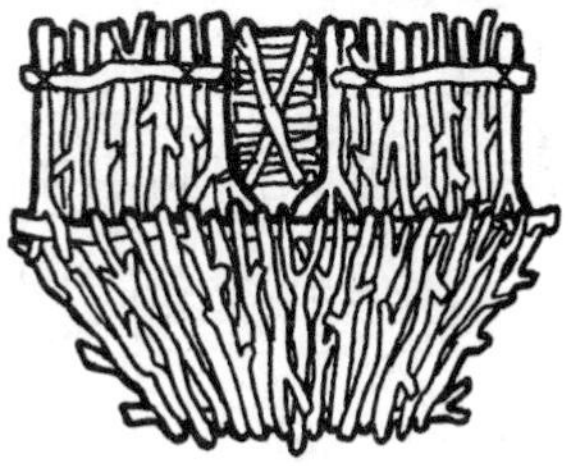

a house of sticks

Word Search

of

y	i	j	o	f
o	s	r	a	b
f	v	p	o	f
m	o	d	f	c
u	z	u	t	w

I found **of** ______ times.
(number)

________________'s

of

book

of of

bottle ___ ___ ___

crib ___ ___ ___

her blanket

her bib

Word Search

her

b	a	v	h	g
h	e	r	e	c
f	l	k	r	h
m	h	e	r	e
h	e	d	o	r

I found **her** _____ times.
(number)

___________________'s

her

book

her her

twin ___ ___ ___

cap ___ ___ ___

chin h i s

nose h i s

Word Search

his

h	i	s	k	h
i	e	p	n	i
y	m	h	i	s
w	z	i	r	c
h	u	s	a	o

I found **his** _____ times.
(number)

_____'s

his

book

his his

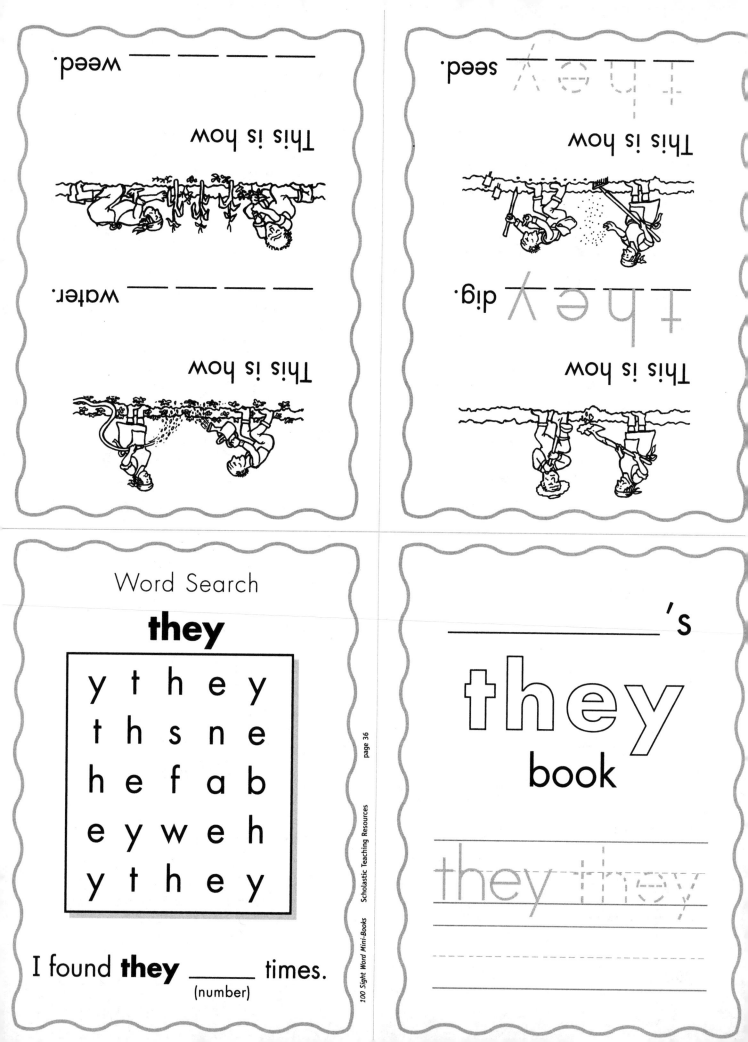

Word Search

they

y	t	h	e	y
t	h	s	n	e
h	e	f	a	b
e	y	w	e	h
y	t	h	e	y

I found **they** _____ times.
(number)

_____'s

they book

they they

This is how _____ they seed.

they dig.

This is how _____

This is how ___ ___ ___ ___ weed.

water.

This is how _____

the cans ___ ___ ___

the bottles ___ ___ ___

the pans all

the pots all

Word Search

all

c	a	l	a	u
d	l	a	l	l
a	h	a	l	n
l	a	l	d	a
l	u	l	o	l

I found **all** _____ times.
(number)

_____'s

all
book

all all

They — — — slugs.

They — — — butterflies.

They a̶r̶e̶ bugs.

They are worms.

Word Search

are

a	r	f	a	r	e
r	b	l	r	j	n
e	n	a	o	y	x
s	a	r	e	c	v
a	r	e	o	n	c
m	e	r	s	u	p

I found **are** _____ times.
(number)

_____'s

are

book

are are

They are ___ the pool.

They are at school.

They are ___ the park.

They are at home.

Word Search

at

f	e	b	t	a	z
a	t	o	s	t	o
j	h	t	a	l	t
a	y	d	t	n	u
t	e	s	g	a	t
c	r	a	t	f	e

I found **at** _____ times.
(number)

_____'s

at

book

at at

I can ___ a spy.

I can ___ a spider.

.

I can be a fly.

I can be a fairy.

Word Search

be

k	e	b	i	b	e
u	g	e	b	s	o
h	m	n	e	p	b
l	w	f	r	d	e
b	e	s	g	a	j
r	o	i	b	e	c

I found **be** _____ times.
(number)

_____'s

be

book

be be

The bunny is — — the bed.

The bunny is — the bench.

The bunny is b y the shed.

The bunny is b y the river.

Word Search

by

d	o	y	b	u	r
k	b	v	i	p	b
b	y	s	w	h	y
p	b	z	b	y	k
m	f	l	v	b	r
b	y	b	s	y	g

I found **by** _____ times.
(number)

_____'s

by

book

by by

Teacher, ___ sheep weep?

Teacher, ___ owls howl?

Teacher, do birds sleep?

Teacher, do pigs dig?

Word Search

do

r	a	x	b	o	s
a	d	o	w	d	o
b	c	d	u	p	m
d	k	o	e	d	o
o	s	a	b	d	y
b	o	l	i	o	v

I found **do** _____ times.
(number)

_____'s

do
book

do do

You can ___ ___
a chip.

You can ___ ___
a hot dog.

You can **eat**
a dip.

You can **eat**
a salad.

Word Search

eat

e	a	h	e	a	f
a	n	g	a	c	w
t	e	r	t	z	e
e	a	t	h	o	a
s	t	a	e	a	t
r	k	u	a	t	i

I found **eat** _____ times.
(number)

_____'s

eat
book

eat eat

This is _ _ _ a squeak.

They are _ _ _ free.

This is for a leak.

They are for luck.

Word Search

for

d	t	f	o	r	g
e	f	o	i	q	u
t	o	r	f	o	r
x	r	b	o	s	y
m	p	a	r	j	n
s	f	o	r	y	t

I found **for** _____ times.
(number)

_____'s

for

book

for for

100 Sight Word Mini-Books   Scholastic Teaching Resources

He can _ _ _ spice.

He can _ _ _ carrots.

He can get rice.

He can get crackers.

Word Search

get

j	g	e	t	i	g
e	m	p	g	q	g
g	u	g	e	t	e
e	h	c	t	w	t
t	g	e	v	u	l
d	f	g	e	t	t

I found **get** _____ times.

(number)

_____'s

get

book

get get

They ___ down holes.

They ___ up ladders.

They go down poles.

They go upstairs.

Word Search

go

q	j	o	p	g	s
o	g	g	o	w	g
x	g	u	b	j	o
e	o	c	g	o	g
g	c	a	o	s	c
u	g	o	s	o	n

I found **go** _____ times.
(number)

_____'s

go
book

go go

Word Search

it's

t	i	s	t	s	s
i	s	i	s	i	i
s	i	s	i	s	i
t	t	t	t	t	t
t	s	t	s	t	s
i	t	f	i	t	i

I found **it's** _____ times.
(number)

_____
- - - - - - -
_____
_____
it's
it's

book

_____ 's

it's

Oh, i t 's so cute.

Oh, i t 's so neat.

Oh, ___ ___ '___ so soft.

Oh, ___ ___ '___
so sweet!

Can you _ _ _ _ _ _ _
it wet?

Can you _ _ _ _ _ _ _
quiet?

sh!

Can you **keep**
a pet?

Can you **keep**
a secret?

Word Search

keep

k	t	k	e	e	p
e	k	e	e	q	i
e	a	e	k	y	k
p	c	p	e	s	e
n	k	e	e	o	e
k	e	e	p	a	p

I found **keep** _____ times.
(number)

Scholastic Teaching Resources

100 Sight Word Mini-Books

_____'s

keep
book

keep keep

I _ _ _ _ fries.

I _ _ _ _ fruit.

I like pies.

I like popcorn.

Word Search

like

o	l	c	h	u	s
l	i	k	e	j	l
i	k	p	d	l	i
k	e	m	k	i	k
e	w	l	i	k	e
r	i	k	s	e	m

I found **like** _____ times.
(number)

_____'s

like

book

like like

He can _____ a mess!

She can _____ a milkshake.

She can _____ a dress.

make

He can _____ a pizza.

make

Word Search

make

b	s	m	a	k	e
r	t	a	u	m	l
m	a	k	e	a	m
a	i	e	a	k	e
k	m	a	k	e	b
e	a	z	e	c	k

I found **make** _____ times.
(number)

100 Sight Word Mini-Books   Scholastic Teaching Resources

_____'s

make

book

make make

___ ___ fair!

___ crayons

no chair

no pencil

Word Search

no

u	n	g	n	o	k
m	o	e	u	t	r
j	f	i	m	n	o
y	p	n	c	a	u
o	q	o	x	n	h
n	m	u	n	o	s

I found **no** _____ times.
(number)

_____'s

no

book

no no

Jump ___ ___ ___ the hump.

Jump ___ ___ the block.

Jump o f f the stump.

Jump o f f the dock.

Word Search

off

o	t	u	o	o	s
q	o	o	f	f	r
r	f	o	f	f	o
o	f	f	u	o	t
o	g	o	z	f	f
t	s	t	m	o	h

I found **off** _____ times.
(number)

_____'s

off

book

off off

wig —— crown?

spots —— stripes?

cape o r gown?

makeup o r mask?

Word Search

or

g	i	r	i	o	r
o	b	o	v	n	a
p	o	r	p	r	d
w	m	s	o	r	a
i	u	o	c	k	r
s	o	r	g	o	v

I found **or** _____ times.
(number)

_____'s

or
book

o r

Panel (top right, inverted)

I p u t it on
the table.

I p u t it in
the pail.

Panel (top left, inverted)

I _ _ _ it in
the envelope.

CONTEST!

I _ _ _ it in
the mail.

Panel (bottom left)

Word Search

put

f	o	u	p	v	o
o	p	p	u	t	p
p	u	a	t	p	f
u	t	p	v	u	t
e	p	u	t	t	k
f	u	t	p	m	a

I found **put** _____ times.
(number)

100 Sight Word Mini-Books   Scholastic Teaching Resources

Panel (bottom right)

_____'s

p u t

book

put put

She can _____ a line.

read

She can _____ a word.

Once upon a time

She can _____ a sign.

exit

EXIT

He can _____ a story.

Once upon a time, by the shore of a big sea, lived a girl who loved to sail.

once

Word Search

read

f	r	e	a	d	r
r	e	s	p	h	e
e	a	h	y	x	a
a	d	r	e	a	d
d	c	l	g	y	i
r	e	a	d	m	t

I found **read** _____ times.

(number)

_____'s

read

book

read read

He ___ the full moon.

He ___ the sun set.

He s a w the sun at noon.

He s a w the sun rise.

Word Search

saw

a	h	s	u	w	e
e	s	a	a	m	k
s	a	w	e	s	s
a	k	s	a	w	a
z	g	a	w	a	w
s	a	w	s	p	i

I found **saw** _____ times.
(number)

_____'s

saw
book

saw saw

He is __ __ old.

He is __ __ new.

He is S O cold.

He is S O cool.

Word Search

so

s	n	y	i	s	o
e	p	j	k	o	t
o	f	s	o	g	x
y	e	o	u	s	a
s	o	m	c	p	n
o	b	l	i	o	e

I found **so** _____ times.
(number)

_____'s

SO
book

SO SO

He can _ _ _ _ a bath.

She can _ _ _ _ a bow.

She can _ _ _ _ a path.

take

He can _ _ _ _ a picture.

take

Word Search

take

t	a	k	e	c	k
a	o	t	u	t	e
k	t	a	k	e	t
e	a	k	g	z	a
o	k	e	r	n	k
s	e	m	k	t	e

I found **take** _____ times.
(number)

_____'s

take

book

take take

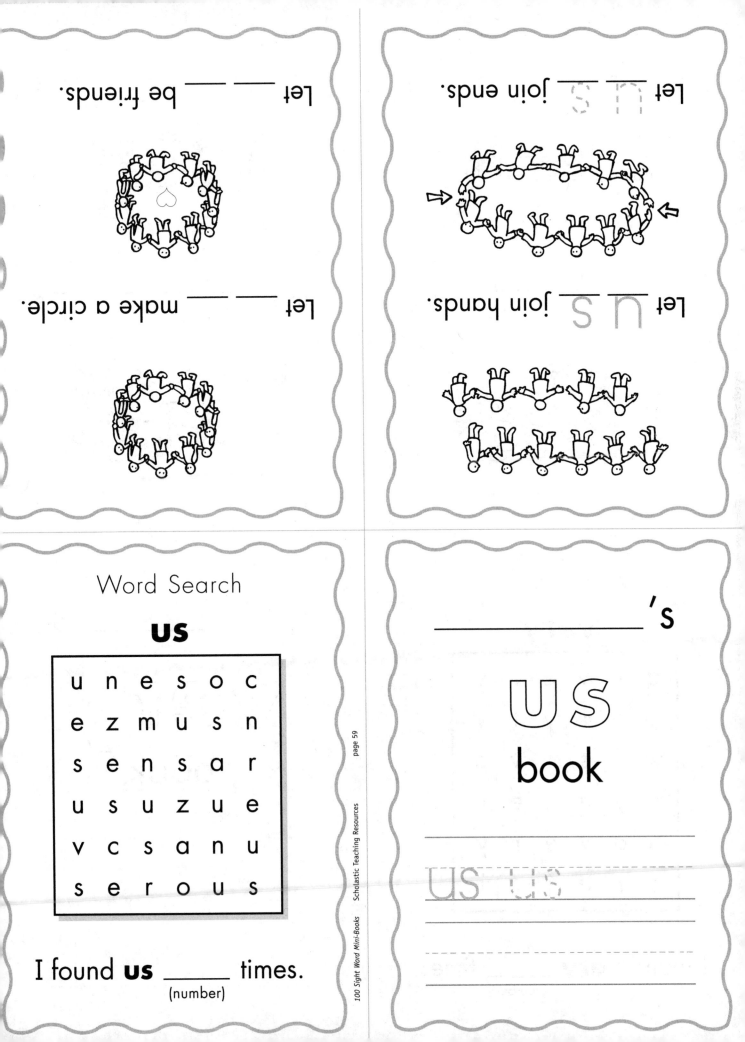

Let ___ be friends.

Let ___ make a circle.

Let **US** join ends.

Let **us** join hands.

Word Search

US

u	n	e	s	o	c
e	z	m	u	s	n
s	e	n	s	a	r
u	s	u	z	u	e
v	c	s	a	n	u
s	e	r	o	u	s

I found **us** _____ times.
(number)

_____'s

US
book

us us

It's ___ ___ ___ rusty.

It's ___ ___ ___ shiny.

It's **v e r y** dusty.

It's **v e r y** clean.

Word Search

very

q	v	v	e	r	y
v	e	r	y	t	v
w	r	s	i	v	e
y	y	n	c	e	r
n	q	v	e	r	y
e	r	u	j	y	i

I found **very** ____ times.
(number)

_____'s

very
book

very very

This car ___ last.

This car ___ first.

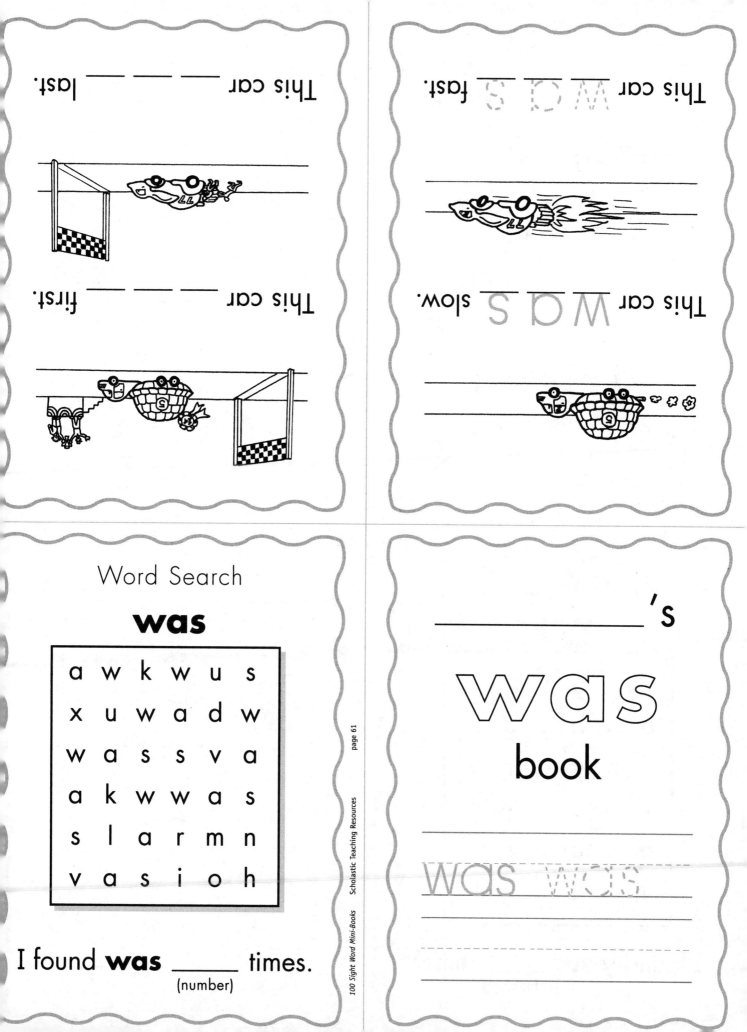

This car **was** fast.

This car **was** slow.

Word Search

was

a	w	k	w	u	s
x	u	w	a	d	w
w	a	s	s	v	a
a	k	w	w	a	s
s	l	a	r	m	n
v	a	s	i	o	h

I found **was** _____ times.
(number)

_____'s

was

book

was was

I found **your** _____ times.
(number)

your

y	o	u	r
u	r	u	u
y	o	u	r
y	y	o	r
o	n	a	y
y	o	u	r

Word Search

your your

your
book

's _____

This is _y_o_u_r_
marker.

This is _y_o_u_r_
book.

This is ___ ___ ___ ___
jacket.

This is ___ ___ ___ ___
hook.

This is ___ alarm.

This is ___ elbow.

This is an arm.

This is an arrow.

Word Search

an

t	a	s	u	r	x	k	d
a	n	m	q	l	s	a	n
c	u	h	e	t	i	f	w
w	a	n	p	a	s	p	e
n	v	d	y	n	a	n	j
d	a	a	e	c	r	b	a
u	n	i	z	d	l	e	n

I found **an** _____ times.
(number)

_____'s

an
book

an an

100 Sight Word Mini-Books   Scholastic Teaching Resources

strong ___ an ox

gentle ___ a lamb

quick **as** a fox

slow **as** a snail

Word Search

as

a	c	s	e	a	s	m	a
s	o	u	w	a	n	o	v
e	a	s	l	s	e	s	q
s	b	r	s	t	u	m	a
n	a	c	o	v	a	d	s
o	s	u	f	s	s	e	p
z	a	s	e	m	c	u	a

I found **as** _____ times.
(number)

_____'s

as
book

as as

You must _____ to the planetarium!

You must _____ to the museum!

You must _____ to the aquarium!

come

You must _____ to the circus!

come

Word Search

come

c	o	m	e	c	e	m	c
c	m	c	o	r	o	c	o
o	n	c	o	u	c	n	m
m	c	o	o	m	o	u	e
e	o	m	e	n	m	s	c
o	m	e	c	a	e	n	o
r	e	c	o	o	w	s	m
u	r	s	c	o	m	e	e

I found **come** _____ times.
(number)

_____'s

come

book

_____

come come

Honey, ———
you scrub the tub?

Honey, ———
you brush?

Honey, ———
you rub-a-dub?

did

Honey, ———
you wash?

did

Word Search

did

c	b	i	d	d	o	d	z
k	d	d	i	d	b	a	i
j	v	i	d	u	d	i	y
p	d	d	o	o	i	b	d
d	i	d	b	j	d	v	i
o	d	d	c	d	i	d	d
v	d	i	b	g	u	d	r

I found **did** _____ times.
(number)

_____'s

did

book

did   did

He — — — — a kitten.

He — — — — a ring.

He f o u n d a mitten.

He f o u n d a quarter.

Word Search

found

q	r	f	o	u	n	d p
f	f	g	f	r	f	n a
f	o	o	o	o	o	x r
o	u	u	u	j	u	n d
u	n	e	n	n	n	n h
n	d	r	d	d	d	f d
d	t	v	o	e	m	e b

I found **found** _____ times.
(number)

_____'s

found

book

found found

100 Sight Word Mini-Books   Scholastic Teaching Resources

They come ——————
the chest.

They come ——————
the camp.

They come ——————
the nest.

They come ——————
the garden.

from

from

Word Search

from

a	r	f	q	a	f	e	t
f	b	l	r	f	r	o	m
r	n	a	v	o	o	x	f
o	a	f	f	l	m	y	r
m	h	x	r	w	n	c	o
d	u	r	o	o	u	j	m
f	r	o	m	e	m	p	f

I found **from** _____ times.
(number)

——————'s

from

book

from from

We _ _ _ fun.

We _ _ _ ted.

I **had** a bun.

She **had** a tart.

Word Search

had

a	h	a	d	l	c	b	t
h	a	d	o	r	d	s	h
a	d	w	h	u	h	h	a
d	a	q	k	z	h	a	d
s	h	e	p	d	a	h	b
a	e	i	a	s	h	a	d
k	o	h	k	h	a	d	l

I found **had** _____ times.
(number)

_____'s

had

book

had had

A bear _ _ _ claws.

A bear _ _ _ teeth.

A bear has paws.

A bear has fur.

Word Search

has

h	u	f	h	a	s	e	g
a	v	l	a	h	z	c	x
s	h	n	h	a	s	b	t
j	o	p	r	s	h	u	l
q	h	a	s	y	a	e	o
m	a	z	h	a	s	g	f
i	s	w	t	d	x	l	e

I found **has** _____ times.
(number)

_____'s

has

book

has has

Sail _ _ _ _ a wave.

Turn _ _ _ _ a prince.

Crawl into a cave.

Come into my home.

Word Search
into

z	l	u	i	o	t	m	r
i	x	t	n	i	c	n	b
p	n	m	t	j	n	h	o
i	g	t	o	q	i	t	v
i	n	t	o	i	n	t	o
d	y	t	i	n	t	o	i
n	t	f	o	s	o	r	k

I found **into** _____ times.
(number)

_____'s

into

book

into into

We _ _ _ _ this game.

I _ _ _ _ the alphabet.

CRAZY 8's

ABCDEFG
HIJKLMNOP
QRSTUV
WXYZ

I KNOW my name.

I know my number.

Danny Moez Ali Julie Wendy Sasha Ting Pat Ruth Max Ziatko

555-5432.

Word Search

know

w	k	o	h	o	v	k	u
k	n	o	w	c	i	n	k
n	n	k	u	k	n	o	w
p	w	o	b	k	k	w	c
k	n	o	w	w	n	u	p
m	o	w	k	a	o	o	n
u	p	k	n	o	w	k	w

I found **know** _____ times.
(number)

_____'s

know
book

know know

Oh, _ _ _ _ .
A moose!

Oh, _ _ _ _ .
A hawk!

Oh, Look.
A goose!

Oh, Look.
A robin!

Word Search

look

l	c	a	k	l	o	o	h
o	l	o	l	o	l	o	l
o	o	k	l	o	o	k	i
i	o	l	l	k	o	l	o
o	k	l	o	o	k	k	o
o	o	k	o	o	l	c	h
k	o	o	k	l	k	o	l

I found **look** _____ times.
(number)

_____'s

look

book

look look

We _____ _____ _____ _____ tracks.

We _____ _____ _____ snow people.

We made snacks.

We made cookies.

Word Search

made

e	m	a	d	e	h	m	e
s	i	a	p	m	k	a	r
m	c	k	d	m	a	d	e
a	m	d	m	e	a	e	b
d	s	a	a	d	k	d	u
e	z	e	d	f	l	m	e
w	k	m	e	e	s	q	u

I found **made** _____ times.
(number)

100 Sight Word Mini-Books   Scholastic Teaching Resources

_____'s

made

book

made made

It is _ _ _ near.

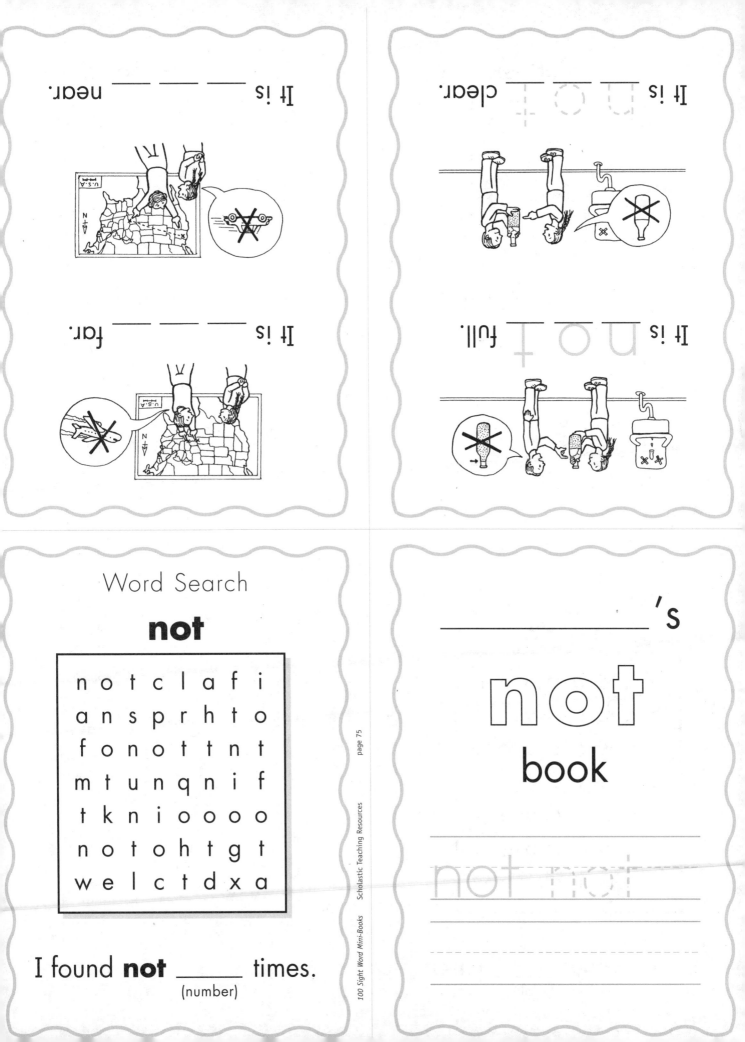

It is _ _ _ far.

It is **not** clear.

It is **not** full.

Word Search

not

n	o	t	c	l	a	f	i
a	n	s	p	r	h	t	o
f	o	n	o	t	t	n	t
m	t	u	n	q	n	i	f
t	k	n	i	o	o	o	o
n	o	t	o	h	t	g	t
w	e	l	c	t	d	x	a

I found **not** _____ times.
(number)

_____'s

not
book

not not

Right _____,
it is smoggy.

Right _____,
it is cloudy.

Right now,
it is foggy.

Right now,
it is windy.

Word Search

now

n	a	e	w	m	n	f	n
h	o	z	k	o	y	o	o
n	o	w	o	u	s	c	w
a	y	e	v	r	m	u	i
n	e	n	s	d	n	o	w
f	o	o	g	w	a	o	h
r	u	w	i	o	t	e	w

I found **now** _____ times.
(number)

_____'s

now
book

now now

Draw ___ ___ wizard.

Draw ___ castle.

Draw one lizard.

Draw one dragon.

Word Search

one

o	m	c	o	o	a	m	e
r	y	r	n	n	u	n	o
c	n	e	e	e	s	r	u
o	n	e	u	j	o	n	e
o	n	e	n	l	o	n	e
h	v	n	o	o	u	e	s
e	c	o	n	n	o	h	e
o	m	e	e	e	a	n	o

I found **one** _____ times.
(number)

_____'s

one
book

one one

This is _ _ _ _ _ mouse.

This is _ _ _ _ _ computer.

This is **our** house.

This is **our** street.

Word Search

our

s	u	a	n	e	r	o	c
n	o	u	r	o	u	r	n
o	u	u	w	o	c	o	e
s	r	e	r	c	u	u	s
u	o	u	r	o	u	r	v
w	u	v	n	o	r	c	o
a	n	r	e	s	a	u	z

I found **our** _____ times.
(number)

_____'s

our
book

our our

"Stuck!" _____ the truck.

"Float!" _____ the goat.

"Cluck!" s a i d the duck.

"Stop!" s a i d the cop.

Word Search

said

s	o	b	s	a	i	d	n
i	s	u	s	i	d	s	c
s	a	z	d	a	s	a	k
a	s	e	s	s	i	i	i
i	n	a	s	a	i	d	p
d	g	d	i	i	i	e	r
m	s	a	i	d	f	s	d

I found **said** _____ times.
(number)

_____'s

said
book

said said

Here are slices.

Here are _____ salads.

some

Here are _____ ices.

Here are _____ cookies.

Word Search

some

n	s	o	n	s	o	m	e
e	m	e	m	e	m	e	m
u	s	u	r	z	u	s	u
n	o	s	o	m	e	o	n
s	m	s	e	o	s	m	s
o	e	o	m	s	o	e	o
m	s	m	e	o	m	s	m
e	n	e	m	s	e	n	e

I found **some** _____ times.
(number)

_____'s

some

book

some some

See the _ _ _ bills.

See the _ _ _
toucans.

See the TWO gills.

See the TWO fish.

Word Search

two

t	w	f	o	t	w	a	i
w	t	a	t	n	w	f	t
o	e	w	t	a	t	o	w
h	w	t	o	w	r	w	h
t	o	v	w	t	o	a	o
f	w	o	t	o	w	t	m
w	f	o	a	v	t	o	u

I found **two** _____ times.
(number)

_____'s

two

book

two two

He can _ _ _ a telescope.

She can _ _ _ an ax.

He can use a rope.

She can use a map.

Word Search

use

u	r	d	u	u	b	t	d
e	s	e	s	e	s	e	e
s	s	e	e	s	s	e	s
u	s	e	d	u	s	e	g
d	s	p	j	s	s	d	m
u	u	e	u	e	u	e	u
s	s	s	d	f	s	s	c

I found **use** _____ times.
(number)

_____'s

use

book

use use

I ____ to be
a scientist.

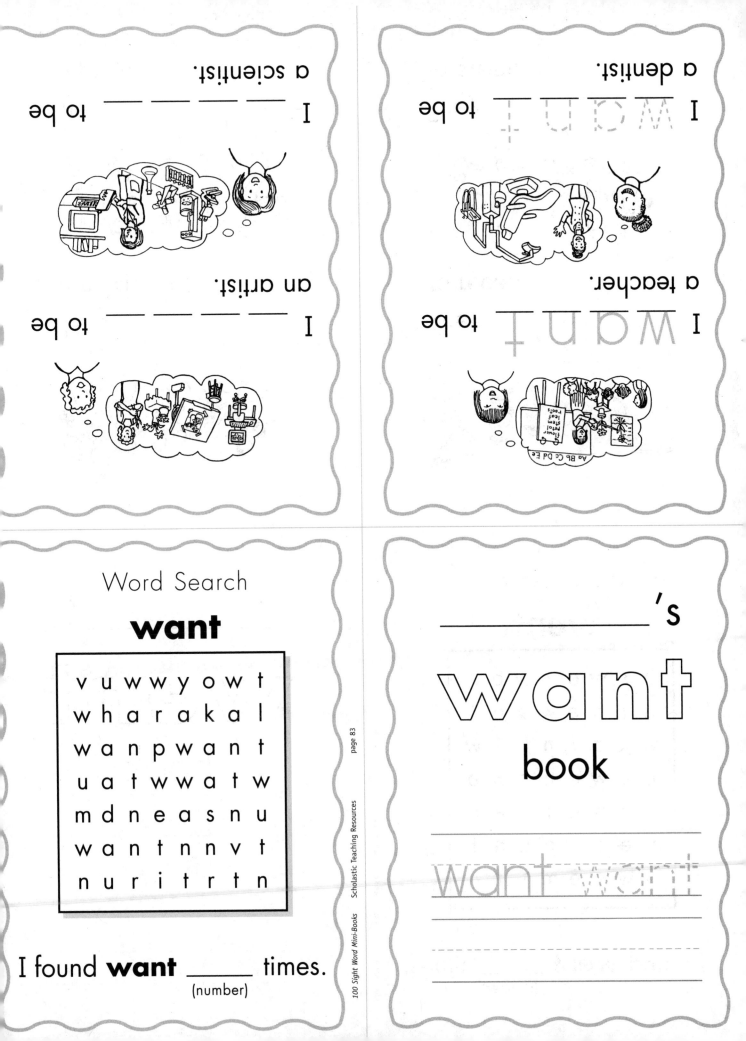

I ____ to be
an artist.

I want to be
a dentist.

I want to be
a teacher.

Word Search

want

v	u	w	w	y	o	w	t
w	h	a	r	a	k	a	l
w	a	n	p	w	a	n	t
u	a	t	w	w	a	t	w
m	d	n	e	a	s	n	u
w	a	n	t	n	n	v	t
n	u	r	i	t	r	t	n

I found **want** ______ times.
(number)

__________'s

want

book

want want

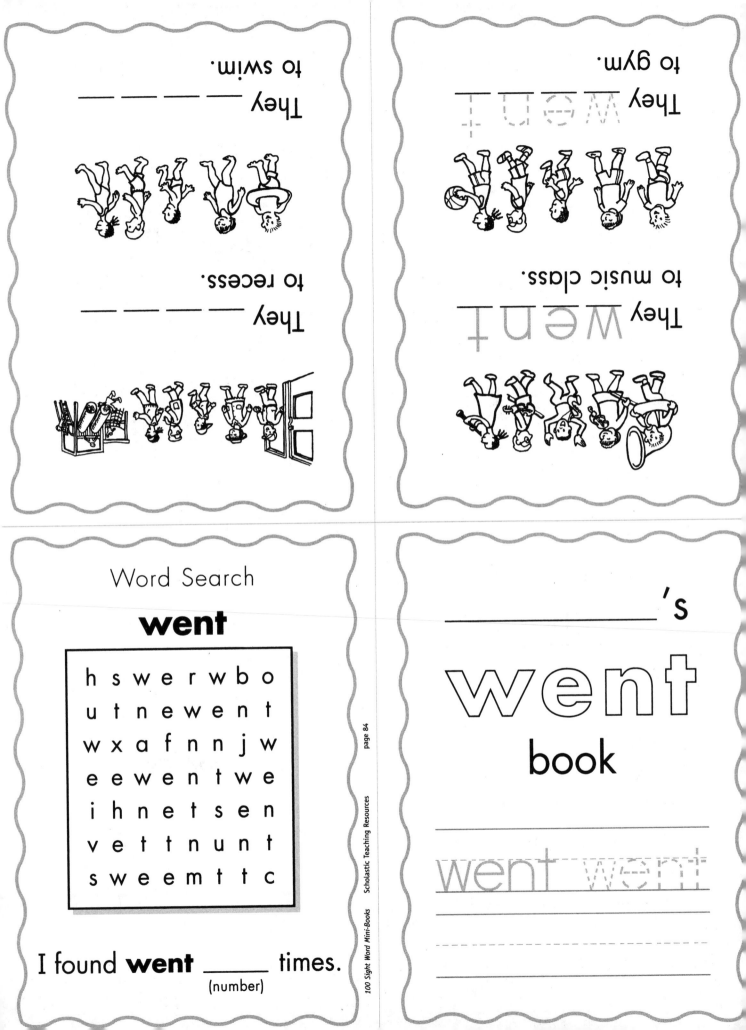

They ———— to swim.

They ———— to recess.

They went to gym.

They went to music class.

Word Search

went

h	s	w	e	r	w	b	o
u	t	n	e	w	e	n	t
w	x	a	f	n	n	j	w
e	e	w	e	n	t	w	e
i	h	n	e	t	s	e	n
v	e	t	t	n	u	n	t
s	w	e	e	m	t	t	c

I found **went** _____ times.
(number)

_____'s

went

book

went went

Oh, ___ a good trick!

Oh, **what** a good boy!

Oh, **what** a good girl!

Word Search

what

a	t	a	t	a	t	a	t
w	h	t	w	h	a	f	w
h	e	c	h	a	h	i	h
w	w	m	a	w	w	o	a
w	h	a	t	w	h	a	t
o	a	a	w	h	a	a	o
a	t	a	t	a	t	a	t

I found **what** _____ times.
(number)

_____'s

what

book

what what

______________'s

will

book

will will

Word Search

will

d	w	i	l	l	m	o	k
t	l	i	w	o	b	r	w
v	w	a	i	i	r	w	y
w	i	l	l	w	l	i	l
i	l	h	l	v	i	l	l
u	l	w	i	l	l	l	t
s	w	i	r	m	o	i	l

I found **will** _____ times.
(number)

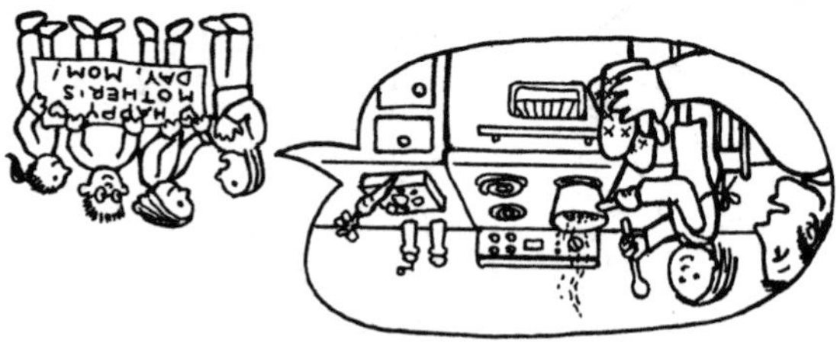

I will cook.

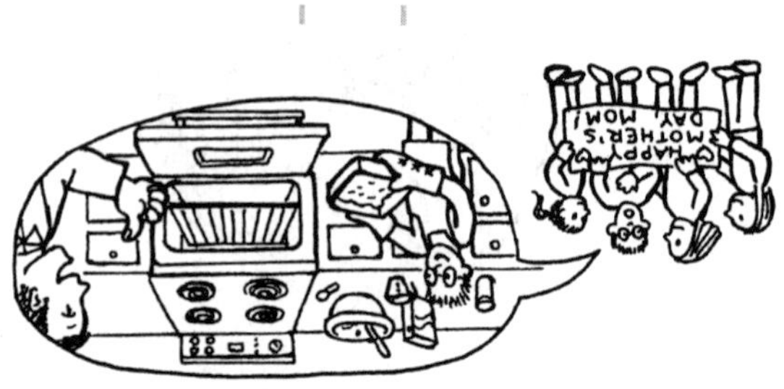

I will bake.

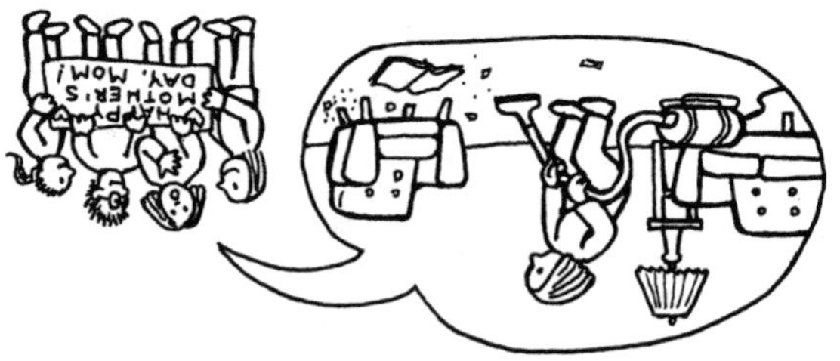

I _______ clean.

I _______ rake.

Word Search

with

w	y	v	e	n	f	w	d
s	i	w	i	t	h	i	r
w	l	t	l	w	i	t	h
l	w	w	h	l	i	h	l
c	h	i	c	h	w	t	c
w	i	t	h	g	n	u	h
t	o	h	i	w	i	t	h

I found **with** _____ times.
(number)

_____'s

with

book

with with

Read a crocodile!

Read a camel.

Read the Nile.

about

Read about Egypt.

Word Search

about

a	b	o	t	u	a	n	t	a	u
f	o	a	b	o	a	b	n	b	t
a	d	u	b	r	b	s	o	o	l
b	k	a	n	o	o	t	r	u	a
o	a	b	o	a	u	i	a	t	t
u	n	b	a	b	t	t	b	f	o
t	a	b	o	o	a	b	o	u	t
d	e	u	t	u	l	a	u	b	i
a	b	o	u	t	t	e	t	o	d

I found **about** _____ times.

(number)

_____'s

about

book

about about

This is ——— the rain!

This is ——— the party.

Run after the train.

Run after the bus.

Word Search

after

```
a s u t f r a e t f
a f t e r n f r a e
t a e a a f t e r a
a a f a f t e r a f
c f e t t t r o f e
a t t n e m e s t r
f e n e r r c r e t
e r s t r a f e r n
c h a f s t r a f e
```

I found **after** _____ times.
(number)

_____'s

after

book

after after

it's a plane.
_ _ _ _ _ _ _ _

It flies

it's a top.
_ _ _ _ _ _ _ _

It spins

it's a train.

because

It rides

it's a ball.

because

It rolls

Word Search

because

b	e	c	a	u	s	e	b	l	u
s	b	e	c	a	u	s	e	n	b
b	b	s	e	n	w	b	c	b	e
b	e	c	a	u	s	e	a	e	c
e	c	c	e	c	n	c	u	c	a
u	a	s	a	r	l	a	s	a	u
c	u	h	e	u	m	u	e	u	s
a	s	n	c	m	s	s	v	s	e
b	e	c	a	u	s	e	r	e	j

I found **because** _____ times.
(number)

_____'s

because

book

because

because

Aim ____ you toss.

Ask ____ you take.

Look before you cross.

Wash before you eat.

Word Search

before

b	g	a	t	b	b	l	e	a	b
e	w	o	r	b	e	f	o	r	e
f	o	n	b	h	f	f	r	o	f
o	f	i	e	r	o	b	o	l	o
r	b	e	f	o	r	e	d	r	r
e	q	u	o	b	e	f	o	r	e
n	o	f	r	e	w	o	b	e	f
e	c	l	e	o	b	r	f	r	u
b	e	f	o	r	e	e	c	h	e

I found **before** _____ times.
(number)

_____'s

before
book

before before

He _____ the floors.

He _____ the rugs.

He _____ the doors.

He _____ the windows.

Word Search

does

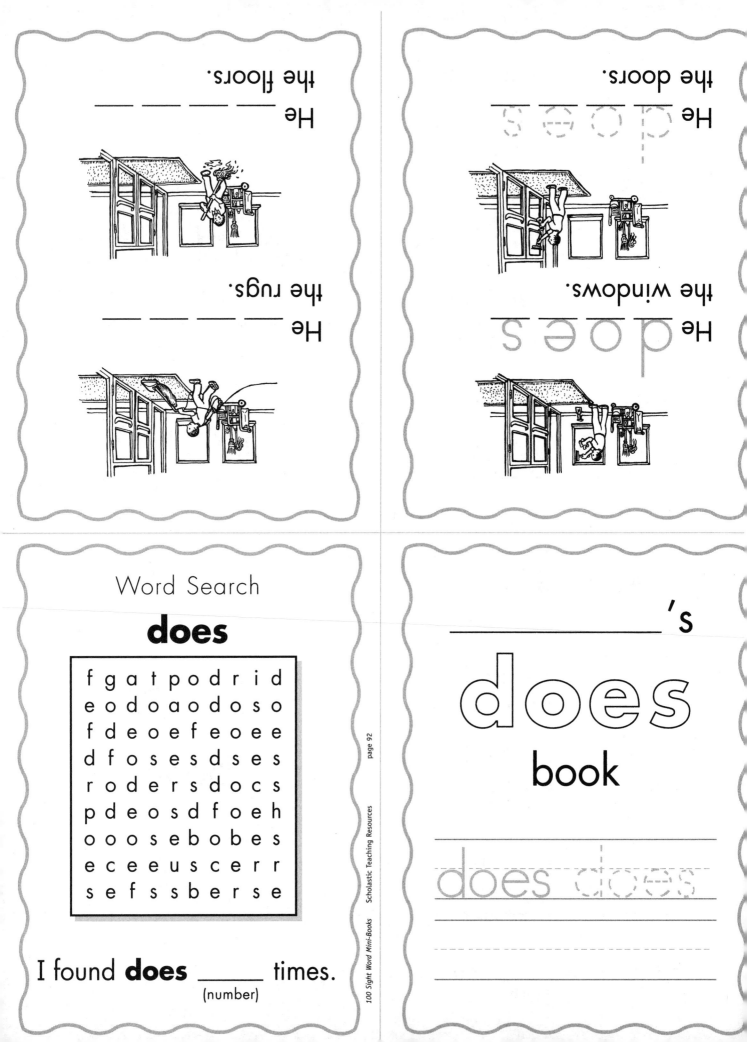

f	g	a	t	p	o	d	r	i	d
e	o	d	o	a	o	d	o	s	o
f	d	e	o	e	f	e	o	e	e
d	f	o	s	e	s	d	s	e	s
r	o	d	e	r	s	d	o	c	s
p	d	e	o	s	d	f	o	e	h
o	o	o	s	e	b	o	b	e	s
e	c	e	e	u	s	c	e	r	r
s	e	f	s	s	b	e	r	s	e

I found **does** _____ times.
(number)

_____'s

does

book

does does

I ___ , like yams.

I ___ , like lemons.

I don't, like clams.

I don't, like pepper.

Word Search

don't

d d d o n t d n n t
d d d a m f d o n n
o n o o b o n t n n
n d n n s a b o t
t p a t t t c o u d
d e o n b d d n t o
o o n s t u o o r n
o o n u f c r n n t
o o o t d o n t t t

I found **don't** _____ times.
(number)

_____'s

don't

book

don't don't

I — — — — my dog a bone.

I — — — — my aunt a plant.

I give my uncle the phone.

I give my cousin a kiss.

Word Search

give

i	g	v	n	i	e	g	i	v	e
s	g	i	v	e	e	i	i	g	v
g	i	s	e	g	i	v	r	v	s
o	v	i	g	i	v	e	o	l	e
k	e	e	i	v	e	r	c	h	r
i	g	o	v	u	g	i	v	e	o
c	e	l	e	t	i	i	s	e	v
q	i	n	c	u	v	a	v	n	i
i	v	e	g	l	e	s	i	e	o

I found **give** _____ times.
(number)

_____'s

give
book

give   give

That plant _ _ _ _ _
over the fridge.

This plant _ _ _ _ _
under the window.

The man _ _ _ _
over the bridge.

The skunk **goes**
under the fence.

Word Search

goes

s	g	o	e	s	g	o	e	s	g
g	s	o	g	e	s	g	o	e	s
o	p	e	r	n	d	o	j	c	a
e	y	s	a	u	g	i	e	s	u
s	a	j	g	e	o	g	o	e	s
g	s	e	g	o	g	o	e	s	g
o	g	f	r	e	w	o	b	e	o
e	c	h	e	o	b	r	f	r	e
s	g	o	e	s	g	o	e	s	s

I found **goes** _____ times.
(number)

_____'s

goes
book

goes

100 Sight Word Mini-Books   Scholastic Teaching Resources

Kites _____ strings.

Chains _____ links.

Birds have wings.

Markers have ink.

Word Search

have

c	h	u	s	w	a	k	n	a	v
h	a	v	e	z	h	a	v	e	t
i	a	h	o	s	d	a	x	y	h
h	o	v	k	a	t	h	v	n	a
a	h	y	e	r	s	h	r	e	v
v	a	a	h	a	f	e	a	h	e
e	v	d	v	n	a	w	e	v	h
p	h	a	v	e	r	h	a	v	e
a	s	e	h	e	v	e	n	l	t

I found **have** _____ times.
(number)

_____'s

have
book

have have

Look, _ _ _ is your treat!

Look, _ _ _ is your dinner.

Look, _ _ _ is your seat.

here

Look, here is the restaurant.

Romeo's

Word Search

here

c	c	c	c	h	c	h	c	c	c
e	e	e	h	e	r	e	e	e	e
b	b	b	b	r	b	r	b	b	b
r	r	r	h	e	r	e	r	r	r
n	h	e	r	e	h	e	r	e	n
s	s	s	s	h	s	h	s	s	s
o	o	o	h	e	r	e	o	o	o
h	h	h	h	r	h	r	h	h	h
e	e	e	h	e	r	e	e	e	e

I found **here** _____ times.
(number)

_____'s

here

book

here here

What ___ I had a crane?

What ___ I had a rocket?

What if I had a plane?

What if I had a boat?

Word Search

if

o	j	v	n	i	t	o	c	i	l
s	u	t	m	e	r	i	f	d	i
p	h	i	f	y	i	z	n	i	v
i	j	e	z	a	f	r	o	f	c
t	s	i	q	u	i	g	e	n	o
i	v	f	c	i	f	i	f	t	i
l	g	i	w	d	i	k	l	a	j
h	u	f	y	r	f	n	i	c	s
f	o	s	e	f	a	v	x	t	f

I found **if** _____ times.
(number)

_____'s

if

book

if if

Poor thing, — — —, eyes are puffy.

Poor thing, — —, tooth hurts.

Poor thing, i̇ts, nose is stuffy.

Poor thing, i̇ts, throat is sore.

Word Search

its

q	i	t	k	f	r	i	s	l	i
c	l	i	t	s	k	t	t	s	i
t	i	i	s	k	t	s	i	l	t
l	t	s	t	r	s	i	c	i	s
i	s	a	l	s	t	i	b	t	r
a	l	h	t	s	n	i	t	s	t
m	i	t	u	l	j	i	n	s	x
h	t	s	w	i	t	e	t	s	i
a	s	k	i	f	s	k	i	s	t

I found **its** _____ times.
(number)

_____'s

i̇ts

book

its its

You _____ wait for an hour.

You _____ mix for a minute.

You just add flour.

You just add milk.

Word Search

just

i	j	s	t	u	d	j	a	g	j
j	u	t	f	o	s	u	u	f	y
u	b	o	n	j	u	s	t	s	u
s	j	a	n	u	f	t	e	g	t
t	u	j	u	s	t	j	r	s	t
j	e	r	u	t	s	u	u	t	o
m	u	n	g	s	a	s	p	s	j
y	u	s	t	g	t	t	u	e	t
r	i	c	t	a	f	w	y	s	o

I found **just** _____ times.
(number)

_____'s

just
book

just just

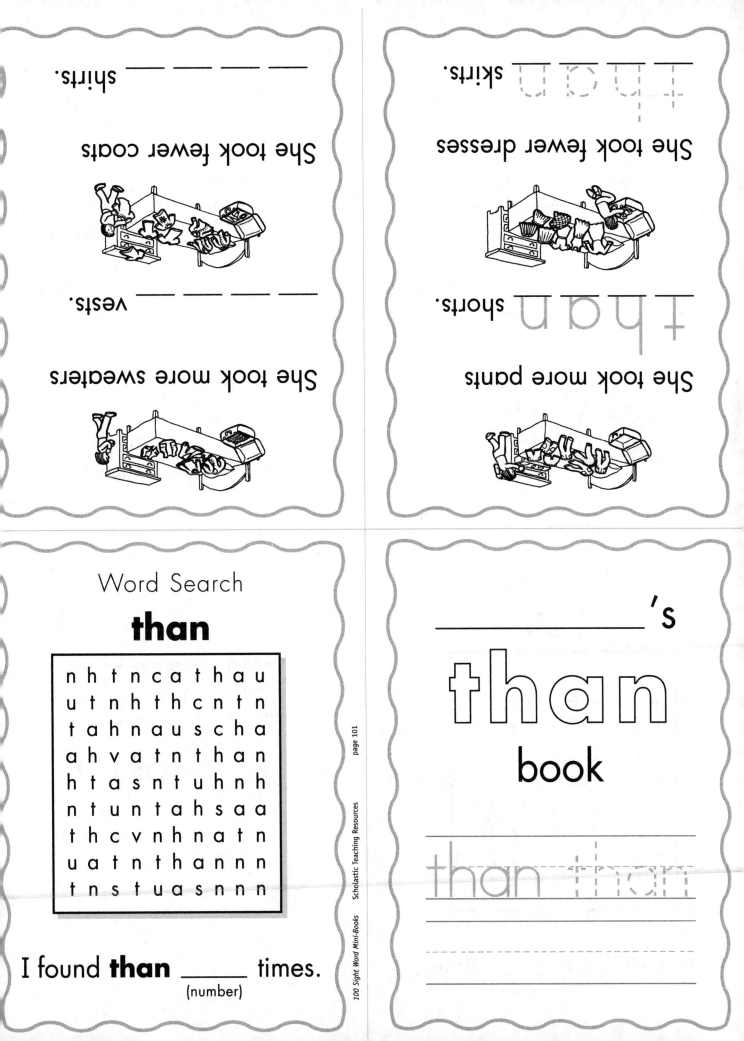

_____ _____ _____ _____ shirts.

She took fewer coats

_____ _____ _____ vests.

She took more sweaters

than skirts.

She took fewer dresses

than shorts.

She took more pants

Word Search

than

n	h	t	n	c	a	t	h	a	u
u	t	n	h	t	h	c	n	t	n
t	a	h	n	a	u	s	c	h	a
a	h	v	a	t	n	t	h	a	n
h	t	a	s	n	t	u	h	n	h
n	t	u	n	t	a	h	s	a	a
t	h	c	v	n	h	n	a	t	n
u	a	t	n	t	h	a	n	n	n
t	n	s	t	u	a	s	n	n	n

I found **than** _____ times.

(number)

_____'s

than

book

than than

This is ___ cow.

This is ___ barn.

This is their plow.

This is their farm.

Word Search

their

e	i	r	t	h	t	e	i	r	t
t	t	h	e	e	r	h	e	i	h
s	h	t	i	f	i	s	e	r	e
i	n	e	h	c	t	r	t	i	i
t	t	r	i	e	t	h	e	i	r
t	h	e	i	r	i	r	e	t	h
i	e	e	t	h	e	r	c	i	e
h	i	r	i	n	s	o	t	h	r
f	r	o	e	r	t	h	e	i	r

I found **their** _____ times.
(number)

_____'s

their
book

their their

Wrap _ _ _ _ in some foil.

Fry _ _ _ _ in some oil.

Put **them** on to boil.

Take **them** from the soil.

Word Search

them

t	k	e	m	t	h	a	m	e	t
e	m	s	e	h	e	t	t	h	u
t	t	h	m	e	e	f	h	e	t
m	h	e	u	m	t	h	e	e	m
t	b	e	m	t	t	h	m	s	m
h	t	t	m	h	e	h	e	t	o
e	f	h	e	e	t	h	e	m	h
w	t	h	e	m	s	t	c	m	t
t	h	c	n	m	m	e	h	t	e

I found **them** _____ times.

(number)

_____'s

them

book

them them

And — — — You tie your shoe!

And — — you make two loops.

And then you pull one through.

First you cross the laces.

Word Search

then

e	n	t	h	e	t	h	e	r	t
t	e	n	h	t	h	m	u	n	h
h	h	e	n	e	e	n	t	h	u
e	t	e	e	n	n	t	h	e	n
n	t	t	n	e	n	t	n	n	t
t	h	e	n	t	e	n	h	n	h
h	e	m	t	h	h	e	n	e	e
e	r	t	m	e	f	e	e	n	n
t	h	f	e	n	s	t	n	e	n

I found **then** _____ times.
(number)

_____'s

then

book

then then

Under _____ is your trunk.

In _____ is your pillow.

Down _____ is your bunk.

Look, There _____ is your cabin.

Word Search

there

```
r e t r t e h t e r
e s h h e h c h s o
t h e r e s e e t n
c h r h n r o r h e
t s e o t t e h e d
e h t r h t h e r e
t n e d e c n e e t
h e c r r t e s r n
e r t n e s t h a e
```

I found **there** _____ times.
(number)

_____'s

there

book

there there

It is — — — bright.

It is — — — dark.

It is t o o light.

It is t o o heavy.

Word Search

too

t	t	t	t	t	t	t	t	t
e	a	o	t	a	o	t	e	o	a
a	e	o	t	e	o	t	a	o	e
o	t	f	o	t	f	o	t	f	o
t	o	c	t	o	c	t	o	c	t
c	o	t	c	o	t	c	o	t	c
t	e	e	t	e	e	t	e	e	t
o	t	f	o	t	f	o	t	f	o
o	a	t	o	a	t	o	a	t	o

I found **too** _____ times.
(number)

_____'s

too
book

too too

They —————— amazed!

They —————— dizzy.

They were dazed.

They were happy.

Word Search

were

e	w	e	w	e	w	e	w	e	w
w	r	e	w	e	r	e	e	r	e
s	e	r	e	s	r	w	r	w	r
e	w	c	w	o	w	e	r	e	c
w	e	r	e	v	e	w	c	r	e
a	r	w	r	c	e	r	w	e	w
w	e	r	e	s	w	e	r	s	e
e	c	e	w	r	a	v	e	w	a
r	e	w	e	c	e	r	s	r	e

I found **were** _____ times.
(number)

_____'s

were
book

were were

This is _____
we biked.

This is _____
we swam.

This is W̲h̲e̲n̲
we hiked.

This is W̲h̲e̲n̲
we camped.

Word Search

when

h	w	e	n	w	h	e	r	w	v
w	e	h	n	k	e	b	e	h	r
a	h	o	e	e	n	w	r	e	n
w	h	e	n	n	s	h	h	n	w
h	a	w	n	e	h	e	w	e	h
e	w	h	e	n	w	n	h	e	n
n	o	c	v	h	e	h	a	r	e
s	h	e	n	t	w	n	e	h	n
w	c	r	h	e	w	h	e	n	w

I found **when** _____ times.
(number)

_____'s

when
book

when when

______________'s

where

book

where where

Honey, where are your shoes?

Honey, where are your glasses?

Honey, ________ are your gloves?

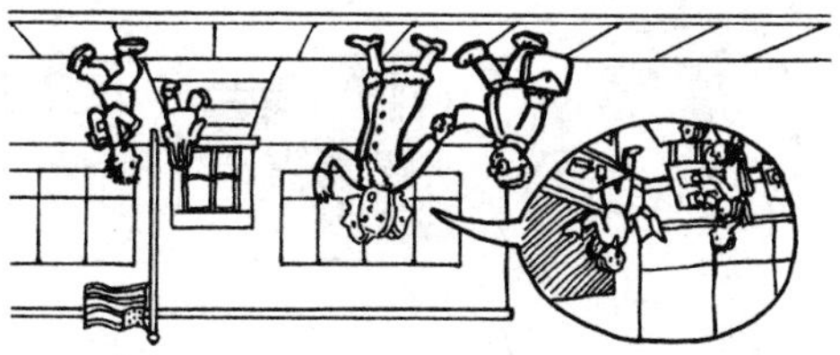

Honey, ________ are your classes?

Word Search

where

w	h	w	c	w	o	r	e	w	h
w	e	f	h	h	n	e	r	o	e
n	h	w	h	e	r	e	k	w	r
a	s	e	v	r	r	m	w	h	c
w	w	u	r	e	w	e	h	e	n
w	h	e	r	e	k	h	e	r	s
h	e	e	t	w	h	e	r	e	h
c	r	w	r	e	t	w	e	h	a
w	e	h	r	e	v	h	s	r	e

I found **where** ______ times.
(number)

Okay, _____ can find it?

Okay, _____ let it out?

Okay, who will mind it?

Okay, who likes gerbils?

Word Search

who

h	o	o	w	h	e	d	h	o	o
s	t	w	o	v	c	t	a	w	h
a	w	h	o	l	k	o	w	h	o
v	k	o	n	x	w	e	r	o	s
w	o	c	h	w	h	o	y	e	b
k	n	w	e	s	o	m	a	w	a
o	w	h	o	n	g	a	w	h	o
s	t	o	c	h	a	r	o	o	w
e	v	h	o	u	w	h	e	t	a

I found **who** _____ times.
(number)

_____'s

who
book

who who

I wonder _ _ _ rhinos have horns.

I wonder _ _ _ mosquitoes bite.

I wonder why roses have thorns.

I wonder why bees make honey.

Word Search

why

r	w	h	e	w	l	y	h	w	n
w	b	y	w	k	h	i	w	h	y
h	l	w	d	l	v	y	h	l	w
w	k	w	h	y	w	b	y	w	p
n	w	y	h	u	p	h	w	i	y
e	p	w	l	y	w	h	y	z	w
k	y	h	w	b	h	p	w	e	n
w	h	y	l	h	i	v	p	w	y
d	w	o	r	w	y	w	h	p	c

I found **why** _____ times.
(number)

_____'s

why
book

why   why

I _____ like to switch.

I _____ like to catch.

I would like to pitch.

I would like to play.

Word Search

would

d	l	o	u	w	d	o	n	w	p
l	w	u	w	o	u	l	d	o	u
u	n	o	v	e	w	b	o	u	h
o	w	o	u	l	d	o	n	l	a
w	w	o	d	l	w	w	u	d	u
h	o	c	u	n	d	o	j	l	e
a	u	u	b	l	w	o	u	l	d
c	l	w	l	u	d	n	c	l	u
s	d	o	u	d	o	d	l	n	d

I found **would** _____ times.
(number)

_____'s

would
book

would would